D1252487

Search and Rescue Dogs

BY CONNIE COLWELL MILLER

amicus
high interest

Amicus High Interest is an imprint of Amicus
P.O. Box 1329, Mankato, MN 56002
www.amicuspublishing.us

Library of Congress Cataloging-in-Publication Data
Miller, Connie Colwell, 1976-
 Search and rescue dogs / by Connie Colwell Miller.
     pages cm -- (Animals with jobs)
 Includes index.
 Summary: "Describes what search and rescue dogs do,
where they work, how they are trained, and which dog breeds
are the best at working as search and rescue dogs. Includes
stories about real dogs who have saved lost or trapped
people"--Provided by publisher.
 ISBN 978-1-60753-380-1 (library binding) -- ISBN 978-1-
60753-428-0 (ebook)
1. Search dogs--Juvenile literature. 2. Rescue dogs--Juvenile
literature. I. Title.
 SF428.73.M547 2014
 636.7'0886--dc23
                               2013001422

Editor   Wendy Dieker
Series Designer   Kathleen Petelinsek
Page production   Red Line Editorial, Inc.

Photo Credits
Mark Rose/iStockphoto, cover; Thinkstock, 5; Daily Mail/
Rex/Alamy, 6, 28; Terry J Alcorn/iStockphoto, 8; AFP/Getty
Images, 11; Shutterstock Images, 12, 20, 24; Aurora Photos/
Alamy, 15; Dreamstime, 16, 27; Jim Frazee/Getty Images,
19; Tom Bear/Getty Images, 23

Printed in the United States at Corporate Graphics in North
Mankato, Minnesota.
4-2013/1151
10 9 8 7 6 5 4 3 2 1

Table of Contents

Rescue Dogs in Action   4

Bred to Search   9

Learning the Job   14

People Partners   21

Amazing Rescues   25

Glossary   30

Read More   31

Websites   31

Index   32

Rescue Dogs in Action

Hunter steps around a destroyed building. An earthquake in Haiti wrecked many buildings. Hunter climbs over piles of rocks and concrete. He sniffs the air. He ignores the nearby chickens and goats. He stays focused on his job. Hunter is looking for missing people. People might be trapped under this pile!

This search and rescue dog is ready to help save people.

Border collies can climb into spaces that are too small for people.

 **Q** Why are dogs so good at finding missing people?

Hunter crawls into tiny spaces. These spaces are too small for people to go into. Suddenly, Hunter stops. He barks loudly several times. He found someone! Rescue workers rush to Hunter. They dig around the spot he marked. They find three teenage girls. The girls owe their lives to the search and rescue dog name Hunter.

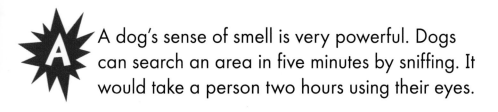

A dog's sense of smell is very powerful. Dogs can search an area in five minutes by sniffing. It would take a person two hours using their eyes.

Bloodhounds are good hunting dogs. They have great noses.

Bred to Search

Certain **breeds** make the best search and rescue dogs. Golden retrievers and Labrador retrievers are strong hunters. So are bloodhounds and spaniels. Beagles do a good job too. These kinds of dogs like to track scents. Border collies, like Hunter, are **working dogs**. German shepherds are also good working dogs. These dogs do not give up. They work until they find what they are searching for.

The best search and rescue dogs are hard working. The dogs must be strong. Sometimes they need to work for many hours. They can't get tired too quickly.

Search and rescue dogs also must be **agile**. They need to move quickly and lightly in dangerous areas. Not all dogs can work in tight spots.

This rescue dog works in the ruins of a factory in Japan.

Search and rescue dogs must be friendly. They should not frighten the people they help rescue. These working dogs like people a great deal.

These dogs also like to please their **handlers**. They do what they're told. And they do it well.

The best rescue dogs are as friendly as they are hard working.

Learning the Job

Search and rescue dogs are trained well. Training usually starts when the dogs are pups. Puppies who really like to play are chosen for the job. Very playful dogs work hard to find their favorite toy. These dogs can be trained to work just as hard to find missing people.

 Where do dogs get trained for search and rescue?

This dog's reward for learning to find a toy in the snow is play time!

 **A** Many states have training schools. They take dogs to parks and forests to train. They train by water too.

Dogs learn to sniff for people by playing hide-and-seek. They practice sniffing out toys. They sniff in piles of wood. They sniff under rocks or piles of snow. Other dogs play hide-and-seek with real people. Some sniff for hidden pieces of clothing. The dogs practice finding things hundreds of times.

Dogs learn to find clothes, like gloves, buried in the snow.

Once dogs are good at sniffing out scents, handlers try to distract them. The dogs need to ignore all **distractions**. They have to keep looking in bad weather. They must keep sniffing if they smell food. They need to be focused on finding missing people. Once dogs can do this, they are ready for a real job.

 Can my dog be a search and rescue dog?

This team of rescue dogs keeps working in the snowstorm.

A Probably not. Search and rescue dogs are carefully chosen for their jobs. They also need a great deal of training.

Dogs and their handlers are good friends and work well together.

Q What are some rewards dogs get?

People Partners

Search and rescue dogs have people partners called handlers. Handlers know their dogs very well. Most handlers live with their dogs.

Dogs work best for people they like. So handlers and their dogs have a strong bond. They also need to know how to reward their dogs for a job well done. Without rewards, dogs usually won't work.

 Some dogs get a ball or chew toy. Some get food. Dogs like to get praise too!

Handlers need lots of training too. They learn how to work with their dog. In addition they need to learn how to help people who have been hurt. They also learn how to rescue people. Most handlers are firefighters or **first responders**. With lots of hard work, anyone can be a handler of a search and rescue dog.

Rescue work is hard. Not just anyone can do this job.

A rescue dog searches for people lost in the woods.

Amazing Rescues

Maddee works as a tracking dog. She found two missing girls named Sammie and Ali. The girls had gotten lost in the dark. Maddee sniffed Ali's pajama top. She then put her nose to the trail. Maddee found the girls, scared and cold. But, thanks to Maddee, they were safe.

Sandy works on a ski mountain in Colorado. He sniffs out people trapped under the snow. These people might be buried under an **avalanche**. Or they might have been hurt while skiing.

First, Sandy sniffs the air. He sniffs for human scents. Then he leads rescue workers to buried people. He might even help dig people out.

A rescue dog sniffs for people buried under snow.

A dog searches for people trapped after a storm.

Do search and rescue dogs ever find dead people?

Sage was a good search and rescue dog. She went to places where big storms happened. Buildings were wrecked. Trees had fallen over. People were trapped! Sage sniffed for people after Hurricane Katrina in 2005. She helped find many people lost in the ruined cities.

Dogs like Maddee, Sandy, and Sage save people all over the world. They work hard to rescue people in danger.

 Yes. Sadly, sometimes the people dogs find are dead. But it is important to find these missing people, too.

Glossary

agile Able to move quickly and easily.

avalanche A big pile of snow that slides down a mountain, covering everything in its path.

breeds Types of dogs that have similar features.

distraction Something that takes attention away from a job.

first responder A person who works for emergency services who is first to a scene of an accident.

handler A person who owns and works with a search and rescue dog.

working dogs Dogs that are bred to do work on farms or ranches; they help people herd sheep or cattle.

Read More

Bozzo, Linda. *Search and Rescue Dogs*. Amazing Working Dogs. Enslow, 2010.

Miller, Marie-Therese. *Search and Rescue Dogs*. Dog Tales: True Stories about Amazing Dogs. Chelsea House, 2007.

Portman, Dale. *Rescue Dogs*. Amazing Stories. Heritage House, 2009.

Schuh, Mari C. *Search and Rescue Dogs*. Pebble Books. Capstone, 2010.

Websites

American Rescue Dog Association
http://www.ardainc.org/

Search and Rescue Dogs of the United States
http://www.sardogsus.org/

Search and Rescue Dog Training
http://www.orvisnews.com/Dogs/Video-Search-and-Rescue-Dog-Training.aspx

Index

avalanches 26

barking 7

beagles 9

bloodhounds 8, 9

border collies 5, 6, 9

breeds 9

distractions 4, 18

earthquakes 4

German shepherds 9

golden retrievers 9

handlers 13, 18, 21, 22

hurricanes 29

Labrador retrievers 9

missing people 4, 6, 7, 14, 18, 25, 26

qualities of rescue dogs 9, 10, 13

rescue workers 7, 22

rewards 14, 15, 20, 21

sniffing 4, 7, 9, 17, 18, 25, 26

spaniels 9

training 14, 15, 19, 22

About the Author

Connie Colwell Miller is a writer, editor, and teacher of writing. She has written over 70 books for young readers. She especially enjoys writing about animals because she is one. She lives in Mankato, Minnesota, with her husband and three children.